Words of Alchemy

Camilla Downs

LOVING KINDNESS BOOKS

Reno, Nevada

Published by Loving Kindness Books
PO Box 19812, Reno, NV 89511
LovingKindnessBooks.com
WordsofAlchemy.com

First Printing December 2019

Copyright © Camilla Downs, 2019
All Rights Reserved. No part of this book may be reproduced or transmitted in any form or by any means, electronic or mechanical, including photocopying, recording, or by any information storage and retrieval system - except by a reviewer who may quote brief passages in a review to be printed in a magazine, newspaper, blog, or on the Web - without permission in writing from the publisher. For more information, please contact Loving Kindness Books at the above address.

"Printing/manufacturing information for this book may be found on the last page"

The text of this book is set in Garamond

Publisher's Cataloging-in-Publication Data
Downs, Camilla, 1970-
Words of alchemy / Camilla Downs with cover photo by Camilla Downs - 1st edition
Summary: A memoir of free-verse poems and prose by Camilla Downs, written to guide her with integrating and processing life's events from 2013-2019.
ISBN 978-0-9800568-4-6 (paperback)
1. Poetry. 2. Nature - Poetry. 3. Memoir - Poetry. 4. Spiritual - Poetry. I. Downs, Camilla II. Title 811.6
Library of Congress Control Number: 2019915414

Author, Camilla Downs, copyright 2019, all rights reserved
Cover Design by Kate Raina - KateRaina.Crevado.com
Cover Photography by Camilla Downs, copyright 2019, all rights reserved
Interior Layout by Polgarus Studio

Praise for *Words of Alchemy*

"*Words of Alchemy*, a heartfelt new collection by Camilla Downs, lives up to its namesake in numerous ways. Downs spans the broad range of nature, healing, love, and parenting, while making sure we have a little fun along the way. And the bridge she creates from the mindfulness of how we see the world at large to the poetry of everyday life is certainly worth a stroll or two across its borders."
- **Thomas Lloyd Qualls**, Award-winning author of *Painted Oxen*

"This poetry collection offers contemplative words, soothing thoughts and peace to the reader." - **Sue Bentley**, Bestselling author of *Second Skin*

"Camilla Downs shares truth, vulnerability and wisdom in her *Words of Alchemy* collection inviting readers to be inspired, contemplate and dive into her world of self-awareness and growth." - **G. Brian Benson**, Award-winning author, actor and spoken word artist

"These poems take you on a calm and loving walk, through the verses of Camilla's thoughts. Alchemy is a perfect word for the title as Camilla understands nature; connecting with its magical, medicinal qualities and beauty which she conveys throughout her poetry." - **Ailsa Craig**, Author of *The Sand Between My Toes*

"*Words of Alchemy* is a chronicle of hope. These poems are an encouragement, especially when we are feeling at our lowest, to keep seeking the light that is our way forward, and focus on the real. This collection is a walk through the positive nature of life. Camilla Downs is to be commended." - **Frank Prem**, Author of free-verse memoir *Small Town Kid*

With Much Gratitude

This book is dedicated with gratitude to the helpers, the friends, the family, and all who have held space for me to be and do as I felt called; so that I may integrate all of me to reach the liberation of my heart. Equally so, to the two beautiful souls I travel this journey with; my children, Thomas and Lillian. I love you both as deeply and unconditionally as the sun loves the earth. Thank you all for witnessing.

Dedicated to those who have chosen a path of the deep inner work to process, feel and release; so they may live an authentic life, unfettered and free.

The Alchemy Collection

Forward	1
The Alchemy of Nature	5
The Alchemy of Healing	9
The Alchemy of Love	37
The Alchemy of Parenting	71
The Alchemy of Mindful Living	103
The Alchemy of Gratitude	189
The Alchemy of Fun	201
Closing	213
About the Author	215
Chromosome 18 Information	217
Team TLC Pictures	218

When the poet puts his foot in that ever-moving river, poetry itself is born out of the flashing water. In that unique instant, the truth is manifest to all who are able to receive it. -Thomas Merton

Forward

Writing has been a sanity saving bridge that has led to peace and solutions. Single parenting two children, losing nearly everything, and choosing to dig deep within, led me on a journey for which I had no map. Through writing, I create the map as I travel this wild, at times unlovely and uncomfortable, life journey.

Writing led me to acceptance of myself and my role as a parent to my two unique and beautiful children. Writing brought solid steps to take with decisions. In some situations, writing was not the only factor; yet, it has been a shining thread of grace that connected my heart and mind along this life journey. And still is.

Several factors led to a loosely held practice of writing every day. When I became a single parent in 2007 I intuitively felt moved to add the practices of mindfulness, meditation, and journaling.

My practice of going for near daily walks also solidified into a committed practice of noticing and immersing in nature. These practices combined with the writing practice opened my eyes and heart to a different style of living, a more focused and connected style.

I wrote the first poem in January 2013. I still remember how wild it felt having these words populate my mind and how compelled I felt to free them. It was the beginning of the alchemy. Alchemy which continues to this day.

Poems have not been the only style of writings throughout the past thirteen years. My first book published in 2012, *D iz for Different - One Woman's Journey to Acceptance*, is a memoir of experiences and acceptance up to that point in time. After the publication, writings seemed to ebb and flow between life narratives and poetry.

The How of My Writing

I can hardly contain the emotions I feel inside when I write. They are as hot as lava and as sweet as honeysuckle, from the tips of my toes to the top of my head. I write while listening to music, or while immersed in the sounds of family, or in silence. I touch my fingers to the keyboard of my well worn laptop. I close my eyes, take a deep breath, and type a few words.

Once the first few words appear on the screen, something within takes over. My heart begins to race with the excitement of anticipation. I become lost in the flow of words. My fingers and hands become warm, the veins in my hands rising like miniature mountains.

The words begin to flow as fast and smooth as water running from a faucet. I type as quickly as my fingers and hands will allow. At times, I notice I have forgotten to take a breath for fear of missing the words that are streaming forth.

Most of the poems were originally paired with nature photographs I made during walks. I would sit to write a poem, refer to the photographs made during the latest walk, scrolling through until landing on the one I knew was to inspire the words to flow.

The Alchemy

Writing is my witness, my soul song. Writing is my therapist, my medicine, my best friend, my parent, and my advisor. This is not to say that writing replaces any of these roles, it simply enhances them.

Writing alchemizes what I experience. My laptop becomes the couch I rest upon; while writing my experiences becomes the therapist. This helps me to synchronize with life, giving myself feedback for these experiences. Writing becomes an avenue to connect with and release the myriad of emotions and experiences of life.

It is through writing that I find myself. It is through writing that I allow myself to physically feel emotions. It is through writing that I connect with the unlovely events of the past buried in my body on a cellular level. It is through writing that I allow myself to feel what I dared not feel beginning at some point in childhood, through to adulthood. It is through writing that past and present events are alchemized and released.

This has been my journey to consciousness, to living from my heart, to peace. At times, I may have skirted the healing that called to be addressed. At others, I walked directly into the triggers, with pain from the past that festered with a venomous poison coursing through my cells and bones. I walked into the pain with fear, yet with love to embrace what part of me feared to let myself know and physically feel. It has been incredibly difficult at times, yet deeply freeing. This path works for me. Your path may look completely different.

For sure, there are times when I chose to bypass certain healing; which may shine through bits of this poetry memoir. When I began this journey, I did not know I was bypassing. I have allowed my path to organically unfold, not pushing myself until I possessed the tools to move forward.

I share this poetry memoir, the alchemy of my journey to date, should there be a spark within it that lights the flame of your healing journey. This collection is designed to be read either in order from front cover to back cover or by opening the book to a random page. Either way, may you enjoy the journey through its pages.

Blessings and much love to you …….. Camilla

The Alchemy of Nature

Earth Dance

As the sun's rays dance upon you like stars twinkling in the night sky, so shall our souls dance upon this Earth.

As you are who you are with ease, so shall we no longer struggle to be who we are.

As you adjust to the World around you without struggle, so shall we go with the flow of life.

As you release your beauty, power, and love for us to enjoy and learn from, so shall we do the same …

And so shall we become vessels of love, joy, and peace.

January 2013

This was the poem that began the alchemy I experienced over the next six years, through writing what demanded to be set free.

In January 2013, I visited Fallen Leaf Lake and Mount Tallac in South Lake Tahoe, California for the first time. Fallen Leaf Lake along with Mount Tallac and Lake Tahoe brought me to tears and I felt as if they whispered to me,

"Come, sit by my side wise one. Feel my power and energy.

As you sit next to me, feel yourself relax. Release all that is not for your higher good. Release judgment and fears."

As we sat together, I felt a healing and was overcome with peace and joy. I was inspired to write the above.

Thank you, Fallen Leaf Lake, Mount Tallac, and Lake Tahoe.

The Alchemy of Healing

Sunset Walk

Hand them over to me
Let them all go

I am the healer
Who is ever here

Open the door
Step into my embrace.

The unlovely
The uncomfortable

Bring it to me
And we shall
Breathe with
It in togetherness.
To further the
Opening of the heart.

It will bring sadness
It will bring discomfort

Yet as we breathe
Through it
Walk through it
With love

On the other side
It shall be known,
A heart opening

Experience this was.

Releasing what
Does not serve
While gathering
Compassion, empathy
And nonjudgment to
Take its place.

I am here for you always,
Mother Nature

April 2019

May You See the Beauty

Pulling the weeds of internal scars
and planting seeds of Truth, I am.

An instrument of the Divine Universe, I am.
A Universe that knows not of suffering and lack.

Yet, I must come to know for myself
that these are but illusions.

These are the weeds of the internal scars
Carried for this life and past lifetimes.

What to do with these weeds?

Either pull them so as to
plant what is perceived as beautiful

Or

Shift the way the weeds are viewed
and see the beauty within the weeds.

Either way will have the desired effect
of seeing through the illusions.

For what matters is the intent behind the action.

In the midst of the illusion,
it feels as if the weeds
will suffocate and extract

the life essence from this body.

It is difficult, this is known.
It does not have to be difficult,
yet, this is the Way few Know.

Yet, one glorious morning;
Sometimes over and over again,
She awakens to discover that she has
indeed been pulling the weeds and
shifting her view.

And the illusion has lifted.

Pulling the weeds of internal scars
and planting seeds of Truth, I am.

August 2018

This poem was sparked by a phrase within an update by my friend, Lalita Simon-Creasey, via her *Soulful Insights* Facebook page.

A phrase of Lalita's flew on love's wings and landed in my heart. This was the phrase … "Pull the weeds to plant the seeds." Thank you, Lalita!

Feel the Joy

Joy, Oh What a Feeling
You effortlessly glide my way
Gently wrapping your wings of love
around me as I become dizzy with
your tingling embrace.

Joy says, "Write about me too!"
I am as important to feel
and be with as are the
unlovely feelings and emotions.

Feel me, physically feel me
Let yourself know that
you are worthy of the lovely
feelings too.

Feel me. Try not to cling
to me. I shall always return
when you allow yourself to be
in the flow.

As a mighty wave
calms and comes to rest
in the vast ocean;
you can allow
yourself to relax into
the majestic ocean of
the Divine.

Practice relaxing

into the vast ocean of
all that is … and know
your oneness with all of
life, with the range of
emotions and feelings.
The lovely and the unlovely.

Yes. Let yourself Know
that you are Worthy and Feel
The Joy …. Come and Relax
into the Divine Ocean.

April 2018

The Way of Pain

Experience the pain, we must.
Feel the pain, sit with the pain,
so as to receive the shining gift
that awaits on the other side
of the pain.

Physical pain, emotional pain,
as long as we push against it,
fight against it, cover it up,
smother it, drown it with
numbing agents, we miss out
on the indescribable beauty
that awaits when we lovingly
embrace it and walk consciously
through it.

Pain is a natural process
of life. We joyfully embrace
its opposite of pleasure.
Pain is simply pleasure going
in the opposite direction.

When we embrace the pain
we embrace the pleasure.

November 2017

Liberation of this Soul

She was tired.
Tired of trying to figure it out.

Tired of trying to make things work.
Tired of manipulating circumstances
to make things work.
Tired of trying to control situations to make things work.

Tired of living in confusion.
Tired of the suffering
created by way of her thoughts.

Tired of the chains that
bound her to the suffering.
Tired of dragging those
invisible chains through life.

Tired of not loving herself.
Tired of not being loved.
Tired of the responsibility of it all.

Tired of questioning her every decision.
Tired of hiding the Truth from herself.
Tired of running from her own self.

Tired of the darkness within.
Tired of the pull of the ego.

What she craved.
What she desperately needed.
Was … FREEDOM.

In desperation she dropped to her knees.
Crying to the all knowing,

Take this tired body,
Take this tired mind,
Take this confusion,
Take this suffering,

She let it all go.
She released it to the divine.

She asked for liberation
from her self-induced suffering.

Liberate this soul.
Liberate this heart.

Allow this heart to open.
Allow this heart to
receive and know unconditional love.
Allow this mind to know Clarity.

Liberation to the graceful
place of Knowing Freedom.
Liberation to the Place
of letting go.

Letting Go
And saying Yes
to Life.

September 2017

Shine

Shine bright dear one.
What your brothers
and sisters think
of your shine
matters not.

You see others shine,
and shrink even further
into the smallness of
not shining your light.
Each soul is meant to shine
in their own way
And no two ways will
be exactly the same.

Your shine is dulled by
years and years
of ignoring that
which creates the shine.

Dulled by messages received in childhood,
that you are doing it wrong,
that you don't know how to do it.

Stories learned in childhood of
how one is supposed to live
how it's supposed to be done.

The light is ever there.
It has not departed.
You have seen glimpses of it.

To allow the light to shine brightly
you must uncover what you buried
so deeply that you remember not
even having buried it.

What you have buried swings
like a pendulum.
One side, the victim
and the other, the judge.

Uncover it you must.
Face it.
Embrace it.
Know you can no longer
be hurt, or judged.

The vital step
of uncovering, confronting
and releasing cannot be skipped.
Fear has stopped you
from fully uncovering
what has been buried.

Eternal joy cannot be
Unless fear is
embraced by we.
I will face the fear
with you.
You are not alone.

Take my hand
and let us walk
together into
the darkness
and we shall emerge
as one to shine bright
and share love with
the world.

August 2017

The Key

When ignored,
the darkness within
slowly erodes this physical body
When stuffed and buried deep within,
it silently grows stronger.

At some point along the path
and at many times,
the darkness surfaces.
Fast as a bullet train
or ever so slowly as a tortoise.
It will not be denied.

Keep turning our hearts away, we can.
Yet, the darkness will not depart
until it has space to be recognized.

The darkness, the shadows,
only wish and pine for this space.
To be seen and accepted and felt
with compassion and deep love.

As the darkness is wrapped
in a loving embrace,
the transformation begins.

Acceptance, compassion and love,
serve to alchemize the darkness and shadows.

Transforming and melting the darkness
into the light.

The darkness may transform ever so
swiftly or ever so slowly.
Yet, it will transform when met
with love and compassion.

The irritation,
The anger,
The loneliness,
The despair,
The confusion.
Surface as they rub
the darkness within.
These feelings and emotions are the
key that allow an
opportunity to free oneself
from the suffering of denying
the darkness.

Freedom to live
consciously and authentically
is the gift this key bears.

Oh, glory be,
the Key of Alchemy.

October 2017

Unearthing the Hurt

She had a dream.
Walking through a
tunnel of books, she saw herself.
Look! Light at the end of the tunnel.

No, wait. The dream shifts.

A vision.
Walking through a tunnel
of darkness, she saw herself.

She had chosen to
go deep this time.
Chosen to unearth
a hurt buried so
deeply, she tricked
herself into believing
it never happened
and was gone forever.

A hurt that caused
her to not trust herself,
to believe she was at fault
for the hurt, and
to not unconditionally
love herself.
A hurt so deep
repetitive patterns
were embedded into this life.

A hurt so deep
a piece of her soul
did eject with the trauma
so as to protect her.

Move beyond this,
that is her truest desire.
Going Within, Going Deep, she is.
The unearthing has begun.

What is buried
has tried to surface
in the past, yet,
she was not ready.

Ready, she is.
The piece of soul
retrieved now,
brought along the trauma
for her to process.

Heart pain, sobbing,
choking, suffocating,
bewilderment, why, why, why,
Anger, Anger, Anger.

The pain of unearthing
and feeling this hurt
is incredibly uncomfortable,
yet, short-lived.

The freedom and liberation
in welcoming and embracing it

are immeasurable.
Free, Free, Free!

The part of the soul
ejected, she had longed to
Retrieve.

This is the present moment journey.

Retrieving.
Unearthing.
Feeling.
Observing.
Letting Go.

Feeling incomplete
she has always felt.
Now she knows why.

The cycle is nearly complete,

She loves you.
She loves herself.
She loves all of herself.
She loves the darkness.
She loves the shadows.
She loves the light.
She loves all of herself.
She loves herself.
She loves you.

October 2017

#MeToo

The Light of Freedom

Time to step into the flames of the fire.
Time to connect with that which you fear from your past.
The past no longer exists and cannot cause you harm.
However, when it is avoided and sidestepped; it does indeed cause you harm.

Avoidance and sidestepping keep you a prisoner of the past.
Held captive to a perceived smallness.
As the flame grows, be still and know that you are not alone.
Be still and know it cannot hurt you. It cannot consume you.

Bring your light to the flames of the fire.
It shall be engulfed and transformed into the light of freedom.
The freedom to claim your power.
The freedom to know who you are.
The freedom to shine your light with others.
Be still. And Know.

September 2017

True Colors

I Love You All.

I love you fear
I love you control
I love you manipulation
I love you conditional love
I love you smallness
I love you victim

You have been there for me
when I needed you most, or so I thought.

You saved me from failure.
You saved me from embarrassment.
You were the vehicle that
helped me live and experience
this life as I thought in my best interest.

I Love You All.

Yet, now I realize
this was unconscious living.
And I now see that
you were not true friends.

I mistakenly called you in long ago
to keep me from hurting.
I am conscious now. I have awakened.

I send you off with deep love

for why we both thought you were here.
It's time and I am ready for
My true colors to shine.

I surrender you all
to be transmuted into
Unconditional Love, Courage, Greatness,
Allowing, and Saying Yes to Life.

Be free my friends. I release you.
Welcome True Colors.
And so it is.

May 2017

The story behind this poem:

- Fear
- Control
- Manipulation
- Conditional Love
- Smallness
- Victim

In December 2016, I had an intuitive knowing that the year 2017 would bring with it a shift. That began to happen in January 2017. I could hardly keep up with all that was shifting for me. It happened incredibly fast, and many times, it was absolutely not fun. It was exhausting as I was BEing in the depths of my own darkness.

I became more conscious of the many ways in which I had been living unconsciously. I remembered, connected, and released memories and events from my past; pivotal things that happened at a sweet and tender young age.

I discovered a freedom, an untethering, a surrendering …. Liberation.

In May 2017, the audience members each received a concrete brick at a Reno, Nevada event by the amazing and talented group, *The Alchemist Movement*. We were to write on the brick a word or words that came to us during an alchemy meditation and to destroy the brick in an earth friendly manner.

The word that came forth for me was "surrender". That didn't make sense to me until the next day when I realized I was to surrender the six, old, and dear friends listed above. This realization brought forth the above poem.

Emerge

And out of the darkness
We shall emerge.
A darkness that
Has been necessary.

A vital and pivotal point
Of confronting the
Shadows within.

For to have more
Than brief glimpses
Of the light,
This acceptance, forgiveness,
And dissolution of shadows
Must be met.

As what awaits is
The eternity of light and love,
Ever there, ever lovingly
And patiently waiting
To welcome us home.

Fall 2016

Forgiveness

It's there
Sometimes we're not aware
The path is littered with debris
of circumstances never fully acknowledged.
And as we are ready to clean
and clear the path
We see …
Forgiveness as the door.
The door to freedom,
The catalyst for healing,
The light beneath the darkness.
Awareness as the knob that opens the door.
A knob turned by the heart of one
giving and receiving forgiveness.
At times we may wish we had not chosen
to clear the littered path
Yet, once acknowledged and accepted
We are free to see clearly
that obstacles have been removed
And we allow a path
of peace, love, and freedom.

May 2016

Nature's Lore

Your grace beckons
The invisible touch of your embrace soothes the soul
The quiet of your peace welcomes all
You are the healer that encourages one to shed what no longer serves
Your beauty encourages renewal with every step in your glory
Thank you for your love.

March 2016

The Alchemy of Love

The Path

Breathe it in
Breathe it out

Look up
Look around

Keep walking
Keep writing

Keep knowing
Keep loving

Hold space
For them,
For you

This is the Way
This is the unfolding
Nature of life.

May 2019

Love Arrives

Love gives
Love receives
Love is wet
Love is dry
Love is within
Love is without
Love is above
Love is below
Love is warmth
Love is cold
Love is stardust
Love is sand
Love is water
Love is ice
Love is dark
Love is light
Love is all there is.

All that appears
Not to be love,
Is simply love going in
The opposite direction.

March 2019

Nature's Way

You see through me
You wake me up
You shake me up
You see me through.

The colors you pair
for these eyes to see.
Reflect my true colors back to me.

With each step
upon your graceful
ever receiving surface,
My love I impart to you.

Focus on a tree,
Focus on a cloud,
Focus on a flower,
My love I give
to Nature with each focus.

Nature's love travels
through this body
to the heart and soul.

My love and appreciation travels
to Nature through my essence.

Walks enveloped in
the glow of beauty,
The shine of magnificence,

Are the Way of loving myself,
Are the Way of appreciating,
Are the Way of stillness,
Are the Way of Knowing,
Ever present Love,
Ever present Grace,
Ever present Peace.

February 2019

The Cosmic Friendship

To have someone
such as you
to hold a mirror
so that one may
fully see the path
she has traveled
and continues to travel.

To have someone
such as you
shower your kindness
and generosity upon she.

To have someone
such as you
to share what
she needs to share
knowing it only
deepens the relationship.

To have someone
such as you
is a blessing
of the highest
and brightest.

I am blessed
by our friendship
I love YOU!

November 2018

Dedicated to my soul sister friend, Carolyn "SongBird" Smith

The Path of the Heart

The path back home
seems littered with
suffering and struggle.

What is this insane
ability to cause
one's self such suffering?

Suffering by way of the
thoughts that dart
here and there,
at times penetrating
the soul as if they
were a cold, jagged knife.

When one golden day
the tides of change
bring the knowing
that the path
is also littered
with Love.

A Love shining remarkably
bright and clear,
suffering seems almost
not to have happened.

The path of Love
The path of suffering
The path of struggles

The path of Joy
The path of Harmony
The path of irritation
The path of guilt
The path of Peace.

All the same path
The path that we each travel.
Made to seem different
by way of the degree of
suffering we endure.

Made to seem different
until that glorious day
that we learn
to love ourselves and
to love one another through
everything that happens.

For the things that
happen will still be;
yet, the perception
of each will shift
the more the one
loves one's self through
the things.

The path of Love.
The path we all
shall arrive upon
one sweet day.

Oh, glory be.
We shall see.

November 17 2018

Love Speaks

Love is silent
Love is colorful
Love is gray
Love rescues
Love gives life
Love carries the
Seed of compassion.
Love lives
For the open hearted
And for the ones
With closed hearts.
Love is always here
Patiently waiting
And loving.

Love,
The Seed Pod

November 2017

The Eternal Flame

Love.
Ever here,
Ever there.
The eternal flame.
Melting the fear that binds.
Be still. And. Know.

Love,
The Snow

September 2017

Love Floats

Love floats
On the wind.
Love brushes
By when one
Least expects it.

Divine love
Surrounds all.
Divine love
Is within all.
All is Divine Love.

At times it
May feel as
If love landed
With thorns that
Penetrate deeply
And painfully.

Bring one's self
Into the stillness
One must.
So as to separate
From the pain.

The stillness.
The silence.
Is the doorway

To knowing the
Pain as the portal.

The portal to
freedom of
experiencing
And knowing the
One love.

Love,
The Leaf

December 2017

A Clouded Heart

And in the midst
Of a clouded heart
And soul,
Love may go
Unnoticed.
Yet, be still.
And. Know.
Love is patient
And gently
Persist, it will.

Love,
The Rock

December 2017

The Call

And sometimes love
Calls to be cradled
In the loving touch
Of another.

Listen to the call
Of love as all
Benefit when
The call of the
Heart is heeded.

Love,
The Rock

December 2017

Broken Heart

And sometimes
It feels as if
The broken heart
Will never mend.

Lo, take heed.
The broken heart
Lay patiently
in waiting.

For the glorious day
When compassion
And unconditional
Love return to
The broken hearted.

For that glorious day
When all the
Broken hearted join
Hands with
one another
To shine Light
where needed.

For that glorious day
When the Light
Shines most brightly,
The darkness melts
With ecstasy
Into the One Love

Of all beings and nature.

Love,
The Rock and Nature

November 2017

Love is Ever There

Doors close.
Control is lost.
Bewilderment envelops.

Yet, love is ever there.
Patiently waiting for
The divinely timed
Occurrences not
Under one's control.

Be still. And know.
Love is ever there.

Love,
The Rock

November 2017

Love Shows Up

Love shows up in
mysterious ways.
Love shows up in
magical places.
Love is miraculous.
Love is mystical.
Love is.
Be still. And. Know.

Love,
The Rock

October 2017

Brother, One Day You Shall Be Released

I feel your pain.
I feel the sadness
that penetrates
deeply into your soul.

The unfulfilled longing
to feel loved,
appreciated,
and validated.

I do not judge
for the hunger
so extreme that
you have chosen to fill
that inner void
with addictive substances.

All of us need this
necessary soul-food of
unconditional love.

I do not judge
for giving your
soul temporary relief
with these substances.

I only send you
unconditional love,

as you are worthy
to receive this love.

As are your brothers and
sisters who walk
beside you in this
path littered with
unconsciousness
and the broken pieces
of your life.

I feel the fear you feel.
We have all felt this
fear at some point
in our lives.

I do not judge
for the hurtful
decisions you
make for I know
your heart is clouded
by these substances.

I send and hold for
you what you are worthy
and deserving of receiving.
Unconditional love.

Yet, you may not feel
this love as your heart is
closed and frozen.

Perhaps in this lifetime
your heart will thaw and open
to the unconditional love
that surrounds you, that is within
you, that YOU ARE.

Perhaps not. Only you
and the Divine know what
your path is to be.

Either way, I wrap
your beautiful heart
in unconditional love.

And there I will hold it
for you until you are
released from the fear
that binds you to
these addictive substances.

I love you.
Your Earth Sister, Camilla.

September 2017

Dedicated to my younger brother, Robert, and all in a similar situation. Since the time I originally wrote this, Robert has taken positive steps to shift the path he once walked.

Love

It's there.
In the stillness.
In the quiet.
In nature.
Everywhere.
Be still. And. Know.

Love,
The Rock

August 2017

She Loved

Ever There

She loved.
She shined.
She let go.

Ever there with kind words,
with encouraging words,
with loving suggestions,
and, oh yes, hugs and happy dancing.

A smile that beamed brightly.
Greeting with open arms all who
were new to this different path.

The originator
of the "Different is Good" slogan.
She checked in on one
just when one thought she
was all alone.

She lived life
to the fullest,
coming to embrace this
different path.

Deeply she loved
her family.
Openly and freely
sharing her
ups and downs.

Dear friends
and family the world over, has she,
who are deeply saddened by her
early departure.

She wanted to help all of us.
She wanted to cheer for all of us.
She wanted to hug all of us.

Every eighteenth of every month
my face to the sky I will turn,
to see and feel a warmth from above,
surrounding me with the
help, cheer, and hugs she
longed to provide.

Fly free beautiful soul,
Fly free and help, cheer,
support, hug, happy dance,
and LOVE for an eternity.

I love you, Susan Moran.

May 2017

My daughter, Lillian Darnell, has a chromosome deletion called 18p-. Chromosome #18 brought into our life family we never knew we had and has blessed us beyond words to describe. The above poem is dedicated to a wonderful mom of another young lady with 18p- …. A beautiful soul who joined the angels in May 2017 …. Susan Moran.

Nature Reflections

All my love
For all time
I share with you.
You reflect back to me
In glory and divinity.
Oh, blessings be
For an eternity.

Fall 2016

Nature's Knowing

As I am in your presence
I feel the weight
Of this body drift
Into the clouds.
My soul melds with
All that we are,
And drifts into the knowing
Of all that is, ever was
And ever will be.
When I'm with you,
The illusion of time
And solidity are no more.
Oh. Glory be.
We are we. We are one.
We are an eternity of
One love.

May 2017

Every Lesson Learned is Another Flower Planted

Thank you Great Spirit for this beautiful Mother Earth.

Thank you for enlightening and awakening lessons disguised as discomfort and failure.

Thank you for the timing and opportunity to learn the depths of true love …. unconditional love.

Unconditional love for self so that I may unconditionally love my children.

That these children who are our greatest teachers and awakeners of our true selves know unconditional love and their worth.

That I may love all my brothers and sisters of this Earth as you love them.

And so it is.

April 2017

Nature's Reflection

Your reflection draws the attention,
even from afar.
My heart and soul know
the language you speak.
Your message forever more comforting.
I love you.

November 2016

Released

The path to love
the path to one's self
strewn with broken pieces
covered in darkness
showered with light
pieces put back together
discarding what no longer fits
like a sculptor releasing
the masterpiece buried in the rock.
Chisel, buff, shine
until one day she is
released from the confines
of the rock.
She is free to know
free to be
free to love and be loved
free to have and free to do
the path to love
the path to one's self
is the longest and
the shortest path
ever traveled.

October 2016

Lilacs

The fragrance you release is light, colorful, and full of joy.
I stand next to you
I lean closer
I gently wrap my hand around you
I pull you close
I breathe in and am transported to the heavens within us both.
I smile.
I slowly release you and pull away.
I saunter away remembering, knowing.
Your fragrance, my fragrance.
We are both love.

May 2016

Blossoms

Your beauty is strong.
Your beauty entices me from the deep sleep of letting life live me.
Your beauty shines the light on my heart
Your beauty encourages and sustains wholeheartedness.
Your beauty imparts strength and courage.
Your beauty is love.

May 2016

Tree Love

Your silhouette soaks into my soul
and stirs creativity to an unbounded place.
I am lifted by your limbs.
I become anointed with the knowing of given talents.
The knowing and conviction of trusting myself.
Your love lightens the load.
What no longer serves is lifted and transmuted by your strength
to float away with the wind.
When I depart your presence,
I leave different than when I arrived.
I depart on limbs of love.

May 2016

Friendship

I do not judge for decisions you make
I have lived through similar experiences as you
I made different choices than you
I do not understand the choices made by you,
that is not for me to understand
I do not judge as I do not walk in your shoes
I am your friend

I see you openly peeling back the layers of your outer self to reveal your inner self
I see you take steps forward, shining your beautiful light and love for all
I see you take steps backward, withdrawing into the comfortable habits and ways of thinking
I see you trying to understand the silence of friendships that are no longer, that is not for you to understand
I am your friend

Yes, I am your friend
I love you
I support and encourage you
You are YOU and on your OWN journey
You choose to do it differently
You choose not to do it the way others would do it
You are YOU and I am your friend

I am your friend
I see YOU, not the concept of you
I love you unconditionally.

March 2014

The Alchemy of Parenting

The Number 18

Today is your 18th Birthday.
Lillian Paige Darnell is 18 years old today.

I can still see you in my mind's eye
as a wee 4 pound sweetheart
as I wondered and dreamed
about your journey to adulthood.

Wow! Did we take giant
twists and turns,
paths less traveled.

Little did I know as I snuggled
you close, sang to you (sorry about that),
and read, read, read to you;
that the number 18 would come
to be a powerful number for you,
for us, in more ways than we could imagine.

When you were 3 years old,
As we sat eating dinner,
As the phone rang,
As the pediatrician delivered
news - 18p-, she said,
missing the short arm of
chromosome 18, she said -
that rendered me speechless,
with tears sliding down my face
into a dinner I could no longer eat.

Little did I know at the time
that this was not the horrible
news I assumed it to be.

Oh, yes. Life changing, for sure.
Yet, not in the way my mind
led me to believe in those first few weeks.

There is no way on this Earth
I could have foreseen how
life changing this would be for me.

Life changing for me so as to
let you be who you came here to be.
For that to happen unconditionally
and organically, I had much learning to do.

Not just learning about genetics,
chromosomes, DNA,
and the effects of deletions of genes.
That was the small stuff compared to
the enormity of the path that lie ahead.

As you step into adulthood on this day
It is my deepest hope that
I have made more decisions for
the highest good, than not.

It is my deepest hope that the times when I have
remembered to share and be unconditional love
stand out and far outweigh the times when
I have not been at my best.

May the wishes you wish come true.
May the dreams you dream become reality.
May the sunshine light your way ever more.
May the moon teach you its secrets.
May the birdsong always sing sweet melodies to your heart.

May you step into adulthood
with iridescent rose gold fairy
wings of the highest and brightest
as you take flight on the next
greatest adventure of your life.

I love you
I honor you
I respect you
I am grateful for all that you
have taught and continue to teach me.

You are You
And You Are Perfect!

Love,
Camilla
Mom

September 2019

Dear Lillian,

I am proud of you.
I love you.

You did it
You continue to do it.

You shine that bright sparkling smile
Upon all whose eyes you meet.

You did it!
From high school
You have Graduated!

You, we, did it differently.
And, that is okay.
In fact, it is perfect for we.

Not everyone is meant
to do life as it has always been done.

This is what creates
the rich and vibrant soup
of human life.

There are those who follow the path
of doing it differently.
There are those who follow the path
of the way it's always been done.
No path is better than the other.
Whether the same path as another is

followed or a different path is followed.

The paths are equal.
Yet the benefit to humanity
is vast in the variety
and depth of ideas,
the dynamic expressions
that bloom when each of us
travels the path of our heart.

You continue each day
in the face of chronic pain,
communication challenges,
depth perception and balance difficulties,
fine and gross motor awkwardness,
emotional struggles,
indecision worries,

You continue each day
with that bright sparkling smile.

You continue each day
Knowing what you want in this life
Knowing what you want to achieve
Knowing how you want to live

You continue each day
meeting all that life has put forth for you.

I honor you.
I honor and support the fierce
warrior within you who

knows her heart's desire.

I honor you.
I am proud of you.
I love you.

YOU DID IT!

Happy Graduation to YOU!!

Love,
Camilla
Mom

September 2019

The Long Weekend

I look forward to these days of respite.
She looks forward to them.
Yet, every time she leaves to spend days away,
My heart is surrounded by a tingling sadness.

It's such an interesting feeling.
When tingling sadness dances with peaceful contentment.
They pair well.
Sharing wisdom and shedding Light.

I take the hands of tingling sadness and peaceful contentment.
We embrace and dance to the tune of an old and worn knowing.

And the small, barely there rain drops fall
to slowly make disappear her wet footprints,
as she joyfully leaves me.
Loving this dance with life
Living this dance with life
What a Life!
Hey, come and get it
Keep it coming,
Get your dance card and let's dance.

January 2019

My Dearest Thomas,

A child called Thomas was born
on this day in 2005.
The child arrived around 9:00 in the evening;
swimming into a new world.

Incredible joy this one
brought along to share.
Smiling, smiling, smiling
a great deal of the time.

A beautiful baby body,
soft as silk, deep with warmth,
and a perfect fit
in this Mom's arms and heart.

The Mom's love and support
for the child, Thomas,
runs as deep and wide
as the Universe and beyond.

What the Mom most wants
Thomas to know in the deepest
recesses of the heart ....

You cannot disappoint me,
You are not here to please me
You are not here to do as you think I want.
You do not have to fear

what I will think.
You cannot disappoint me.

This Mom will support you
always and forever,
beyond even the time in
which she is using this body.
This Mom's love is not
conditioned on who you be or don't be,
nor what you do or don't do.
This Mom trusts you.
This Mom believes in you.
This Mom knows you are worthy
of your heart's desire.
This Mom apologizes for
conditions not being as you
and she would like.

You cannot disappoint me.
I will love and support you
always and forever ...

Happy 13th Birthday Thomas!

I love YOU!!

November 13 2018

My Dearest Lillian,

I wish for you the happiest of birthdays.
I wish for you a joyful and peaceful 17th trip around the sun.
I wish for you all the experiences
That your heart desires.

Walks with you, I truly treasure.
Creating art with you, I truly treasure.

Laughing and being silly with you, I truly treasure.
May strength, courage, peace and kindness be with you always
and forever ....
As will my Love.

I Love You!!

Camilla
Mom
xoxo

September 2018

Knowing of the Heart

We have come together upon this Earth
to travel our own separate paths
Yet, traveling them together.

It has not escaped my attention
that there were and are places
and events we talked and
dreamed of experiencing.

Our lives together seem to
have become mundane and boring.

Seeming to have the same days
over and over again.
With little new experiences
by way of sights, sounds,
and adventures.

Sadness and failure encroached
upon these shoulders and heart
As the message was received
of how important it is to
travel with one's family.

Travel so as to have one to one
time together … away from the
normalcy of being in the
same place and routines.

Yet, before the cloud could

fully envelop this heart,
the heart whispered to
the sadness a response
so profound and enlightening
the sadness and failure
did halt and lift to be
transmuted to peace and knowing.

The heart whispered ...
Wait.

Each walk taken,
Each drive around
neighborhoods,
Each date day,
Each spontaneous trip
for simple life's
necessities,
Each trip to the park,
Each drive to a lookout
to watch the sunset or
have a car picnic,
Each occasion you chose
to make special ...
Each of those times was
a trip to a beautiful
and everlasting destination.

You and your children
have taken many trips.
They may not be the
actual destinations the

three of you envisioned.

No. They are not.

Yet, each of these trips
led to destinations
that many may never get
a chance to experience.

The trip. The destination.
Within you it is.
Take it with you
always, you do.
This is the alchemy
of the heart.

Glory be.
Take notice of
your profound ability
to make something
out of seemingly nothing.

Know this.
And be free.
Hallelujah!

June 2018

Dedicated to my children ... Thomas and Lillian

There's nothing better than a walk with my loves. I cherish every walk taken with each one of them. Every walk …. Since they were wee tiny ones growing within me. As of the writing of the previous poem, Lillian and I have taken walks together for nearly 17 years; and Thomas and I for nearly 13 years. Love, sweet love.

What if it Were You

He's frustrated
He's not sure how to handle it.

He lashes out
He says unkind words
He insults
He teases.

He's not sure how to handle it.
He's frustrated.

The mom tells the son
that it is okay to
have these feelings.
Feeling angry, sad,
frustrated is okay.
These feelings are valid
simply because he has them.

He does not understand
why the sister behaves
the way she does.
Does not understand
the inflexibility.
Does not understand
the fears she harbors.
Does not understand
the massive and, at times,
violent meltdowns.
Does not understand

the anxiety that
can lead to a meltdown.

He becomes critical
and desires something
be done about the situation.
He feels the mom blames
the missing genes
for the sister's behavior.
He feels that the mom blames
him for being angry and upset.

The mom lets him know
that it is okay for
him to be feeling this way
He is not wrong for
feeling frustrated
and angry.

The mom only asks him
to think about this ...

What if you were her?
What if ...

You could not speak clearly so that others understand you?
You were in near constant pain almost every single day?
You had balance issues and fell constantly?
You were much, much shorter than your peers?
You were much, much shorter than your *younger* sibling?
Your body did not cooperate with accomplishing tasks?
You could not easily use a spoon or butter knife?

You could not drink from a glass without a straw?
You could not easily brush or floss your teeth?
You were the one without lip closure?
You were the one with hand tremors?
You were the one with fine motor skill difficulties?
You were riddled with anxiety and irrational fears?
You were the one with an entire section of your 18th chromosome missing?

What if this were you
and not the other?

The mom was not telling him
that these difficulties
are excuses for being
unkind to others.

Simply to ponder
what one's life would
be like if all that is
easy and simple vanished …

Ponder if it all became
difficult and a struggle …

Simply ponder …

The mom let him know he
could continue to feel
and believe what he chooses.

The mom will not force

her opinions of
the situation upon him.

The mom simply asks him to ponder.

And the mom will ponder
what it would be like

if she were the sibling
to the one ...

The mom simply asks him to ponder.

And they shall ponder.

April 2018

Dearest Thomas

May you always ask questions,
May you always engage others in conversation,
May you always seek to understand.

May you ever know there are times when silence is the Way.

May you continue to be an explorer in the sea of knowledge,
May you filter that knowledge through the knowing of the Heart,
May you love this life and live it to the fullest.

May you ever be connected to the knowing of your Heart,
May you ever still hold compassion for all beings, animals, and plant life,
May you ever hold the desire to advocate for what speaks to your Heart.

May you always be aware of your connection to Nature,
May you always continue to explore Nature's beauty,
May you always see the beauty when others see it not.

May you ultimately discover that all the answers lie within You.
May you continue to yearn for walking the trails and woods of Nature,
May the peace and warm feelings instilled by this continue to fall upon you as gently as snowflakes fall upon the grass.

May happiness and joy ever be woven into your life,
May happiness and joy sprout in every nook and cranny of your days,
May you always be reassured that all is happening as it should and all is okay.

May you ever stay true to the compass of your Heart.
May you ever know that the Heart is where my love for you resides,
May you ever know that my love is eternal, throughout all of time, and all dimensions.

I love you,
Camilla
Mom
xoxo
January 2018

For Thomas as a 2017 Christmas gift

Dearest Lillian

May you always live with an open and light heart,
May you always live knowing you are unconditionally loved,
May you always live knowing and allowing peace, joy, and abundance.

May good fortune smile and shower upon you,
May joy stalk you and be hidden in every nook and cranny of your life,
May peace float always above you as a puffy cloud in a bright blue sky.

May the shadows ever be there to bring delight and laughter to your world,
May the rays of the sun ever bring a smile and tender joy to your life,
May you never lose your sense of wonder with all things that most have lost.

May you always hear the sweet sound of the magical bell.

May you always know, even after I am long done with this body,
that my love for you is eternal and never ending.

I love you,
Camilla
Mother
xoxo

December 2017

For Lillian as a 2017 Christmas gift

Thomas ....

In this, your twelfth year
orbiting the sun ....

You light up my life
like I could never
have imagined ....

For I fully believe
you and I have a long
history beyond the
earth suits we now wear.

You and I made an
agreement to help
one another past
blocks that we've
held onto for
many lifetimes.

Thank you for staying
true to our long
ago made agreement.

As much and as many
times as I'd like
to stick my head
in the sand and
pretend I don't know
what I know.

Thomas Arthur ….
My soulmate from
another time, another place.
You are one
who truly
knows me.

Knows me enough ….
to call me on
my own BS.
Standing up to me
when the ego
rears its nastiness.

You came swimming
into this world
on the thirteenth
of November 2005,
and have known
from the moment
of your first breath
who you are …
And have never
forgotten to stay
true to your heart.

Yet, you remind
me often that you
too are human …
With unkind
remarks and
decisions.

Indeed a reminder
of the Yin and Yang
of this wondrous
thing called Life.

I am so
incredibly blessed
by having you
as a partner in
this dance of life.

In other words ... You are Unforgettable and I Love YOU!!

November 2017

The Dance of Lillian

She came into this world
with her own agenda.
She came missing the short
arm of chromosome number 18.

Never mind what they
thought about how
they would parent her.

They would quickly
learn no parenting
manual existed for
the lessons she was
to bring with her
through this incarnation.

She delivered the
gift of shattered
expectations early
in her Earth life
as Lillian.

She had chosen
as a mom someone
who had many uncomfortable
lessons to learn.

Patience was to
be another of the
lessons she brought

with the tiny little
body she inhabited.

She was not done yet.
The next gift delivered
flowed into their
lives as a pure
cold stream runs
through the land.

That message.
Acceptance.

Acceptance of what life
had delivered and would
deliver.

This little bundle
that grew into a bright
shining light had
many lessons bundled within.

The next was to be
release of judgments.
Oh. That one stung
worse than a
bee sting on a warm
sunny day. A sting
that lingered for
years, resurfacing
at just the right moment.

This little bundle
who could be anything
but a bundle of joy.
A bundle of anger,
anxiety, violence, and
all kinds of negativity.

With this bundle
came the lesson of
living in the present
moments of life.
Being mindful and
learning the art
of mindfulness.

Responding to this one
from the present moments
of life instead of hurts
from the past. Oh. This
was one of the hardest
lessons yet.

This had nothing to do
with this little bundle,
now a blossoming teen.
As she may have come
into this world in all
her nakedness.

Yet, she contained in
the fibers of her very
being, a Divinely pure

mirror that served to reflect
to the one called Mom
the lesson that it
was she who needed
to go within, to
confront her past,
to feel what she had
not wanted to feel,
And release it.

This would be the Mom's
lesson of learning how to
live in the present moments
of life and to embrace the
art of mindfulness.

Four pounds and five
ounces of life changing,
life altering, life correcting
joy arrived on the evening
of September 14, 2001.

Gratitude does not
even begin to describe
what the Mom feels about
the tiny bundle and she
deciding to have these
roles in this life.

The blossoming teen
was the catalyst
to teaching the mom that

she had it all wrong.
She and all children
are our awakeners.
They are not to
be pushed to the side,
put in the corner,
talked down to,
treated harshly,
abused, controlled,
barked at with commands
and "because I said so"
Ridiculousness.

They are to be
respected and
treated as equals.
They may inhabit tiny
little bodies when they
first arrive.

Yet, the souls within
these tiny precious bodies
have much to teach us.
She came in missing
the short arm of her
chromosome number 18.

The lesson that encompasses
all of the other lessons
she brought forth.

Different.

She taught the mom
that she was going to be
the one who lives life
Differently.

Mom learned how to live
life from the heart,
trusting the whisperings
of the heart.

She, who now enters
her sixteenth orbit
around the sun in this
Lillian body.

Happy, Happy Birthday
YOU beautiful being.
Thank you for blessing me
and being my awakener.

I Love You,
Camilla
Your Earth Mom

October 2017

The Alchemy of Mindful Living

Un Doing

Speak your truth dear one
with a golden tongue

let it be known
your true self

ride the times of the wind
listen to the longing of your heart

slow down the drum beat
of the must be doing

listen to the melody
of relaxation as it
plays ever more
in your bones

when this is allowed
when this is welcomed
what is truly of your
concern will rise to the surface

do as you must
do as you are compelled
be concerned not
with what others
think of you and your actions

be free and relax
into the knowing
of your heart and soul
into the truth of your cells and bones

speak your truth dear one
with a golden tongue
and free yourself.

June 2019

Sun Wishes

Went for a walk
Made a wish
Drew in a breath
Pursed my lips
Blew the wish
On waves of wind
To the loving
Embrace of the sun.

April 29 2019

It was a long walk today. What a beautiful walk it was. Light, free, joyful. Listened to the birdsong. Felt the warmth of the sun and the lovely breeze. Smelled lilacs. Tasted my true self. Sensed newness in my bones. What a beautiful walk it was.

One Way

Stop the madness.
Time to remember.
These thoughts are not
one's true essence.

These thoughts are of the mind.
Stories of the past,
Patched together with
the glue of unlovely memories.

They are not true in the now.
They are but illusions,
sparkles and dust of the past.

Recognize the
True You as the
one in observation
of these thoughts.

Take a deep
cleansing breath,
purse the lips,
blow
and
clear them
from one's heart.

Acknowledge them,
Feel them,
Embrace them,

Love them.

Release these mind stories
of the past.
It is time.
Release the torture.

I deserve this.
You deserve this.
We deserve this.
And we are free.

February 2019

The Lure of Words

A love of reading
A love of books
A love of the written word
She has always had.

Devouring one
book after another
after another.

Books here.
Books there.
Books everywhere.
Oh, the sight, the feel,
the sound, the smell.
Intoxicating to even imagine.

Deliberately walking the aisle
of the library,
of the book store,
she feels at home.

Perusing the titles,
gently taking hold of
the book's spine,
sliding it from the shelf,
slowly running her
fingertips across
the book's title,
opening the book,
lifting the opened book

to her nose and
inhaling the unique
scent only a book can radiate.

Simply holding, feeling, and
smelling a book
sends here straight away
to other worlds, lands,
and journeys.

When finally opening
the book to begin
the adventure,
a palpable,
stomach tingling
Excitement lures her
to the pages.

This has been the way.
A beautiful way.
A way that led her
to know she was to
write, she was to let
black words flow forth
and fill the white pages,
one after another
after another.

She laughs words
She exhales words
She cries words
She bleeds words

She dances words.

She swallows the words
of life to be mixed and
meshed with her essence.

Magically, as if under a spell,
she releases the words
from her mind's eye
fast as lightning through
her fingertips onto the screen.

Books, books, books.
Words, words, words.

Words are oxygen
Words are food
Words are water
Words are shelter
Words are life.

Her teacher
Her friend
Her lover
Her mentor
Books are these,
and more,
to she.

A love of reading
A love of books
A love of the written word

She has always had.

Devouring one
book after another
after another.

All the while
the words,
the books,
devoured she.

January 2019

The Ride of Life

No longer riding on the merry-go-round,
She celebrates whenever she wants,
She laughs when it's funny,
And sometimes when it's not funny,
She cries when the tears want to flow,
She eats breakfast for dinner,
She dances in the aisles,
She hands out hugs
Like Halloween candy,
She hugs the trees,
She meets her edge,
She stays with the experiences of life,
She lives.
And so it is.

December 2018

When Life Comes Together

And she began the walk
The walk of only she,
breathing in, knowing she was breathing in
breathing out, knowing she was breathing out

She listened to the sounds of
the stillness
the bird songs
the beeping construction equipment
the roar of an airplane overhead
the creak and pop of the plastic fence
the screech of the vulture as he took flight
the long distance cough of another echoing across the wetland
the jingle of her earrings in the breeze
the whir of the traffic in the distance

She felt the soft breeze
brush her cheeks
lifting her hair ever so gently.

She focused
her eyes on the vibrant pink flower
and found her thoughts to be ....

I am the flower swaying in the breeze
The flower is me

She focused her eyes on the crisp green
blades of grass hosting plump round droplets
of water

I am the blade of grass hosting the water droplets
the blade of grass is me

I am the water droplet resting on the blade of grass
the water droplet is me

She focused her eyes on the majestic vulture

I am the vulture resting on a rock
The vulture is me

She focused her eyes on and lay her hands upon
the crooked and tall tree.

I am the tree standing crooked and tall
the tree is me

And she is,
and they are,
fulfilling life.

And she ended the walk
The walk of the One.
breathing in, knowing she was breathing in
breathing out, knowing she was breathing out.

October 27 2018

Water Dance

As the sun's reflection
Becomes a dancer
Of the water,
She takes by the hand
the one who walks.

She whispers sweet reminders,
To the walker's heart.

She dances elegantly.
She dances of love and grace.
She dances unknown
To many who see her
Only with the eyes.

For those that catch
Glimpses of her water dance
Life loses the illusions
of trickery.

She dances to
Guide them in
Remembering what
Their hearts continue
To know.

She reminds them
They are all different.
Yet, they are all the same.
We are they.

They are we.

The hand she
Took the walker by
Melts into the Sun.
The Sun swallows her
And she swallows the Sun.
They become One.

The one who walks
continues her
Walk of life
Having been reminded
Of what the brain had clouded.
Yet.
What the heart always knows.
And lo, freer and lighter, she continues to Walk.

September 2018

Cloud Whisperings

The eyes cannot possibly see the depth of your beauty.
The heart beats with the Knowing.
The nostrils inhale breath with the Knowing.
The mouth speaks the Knowing, laced within every word spoken.
The ears hear the birdsong of the Knowing.
For the depth of your beauty is this same Knowing.

August 2018

Headed Home

And she walked.
And she walked.
She walked until
Arriving at
The home of
Peace and Joy.
Discovering once there,
She had been
Here all along.

August 2018

The Silence

The cawing of the seagulls overhead.
The beep and roar of the construction equipment.
The call and honk of the geese.

The thunder of the leaf blower.
The slow ripples in the lake.
The ever so gentle harmony of the song birds.

The blare of horns in the distance.
The melodic quack of the duck.
The squawking of the coot.

I close my eyes and I become one with all.
I lose the feeling of this body and meld with
the oneness of all that surrounds me.

This is life.
This is love.
And so it is.

June 1 2018

The Space Within

There is a space within
A space occupied, it was.

Occupied with judgment
Occupied with harshness
Occupied with unkind thoughts
towards others.

There is a space within
where the darkness
of judgment used to live.

Judgment lives
here no more.
Evicted.
It has been.

There is a space within.

A soft space of love
of compassion
of empathy
of understanding.

For a journey
of thousands of miles
has been lived with
the understanding

that each one of us
has traveled a similar journey.

To be sure,
not the same journey.
No, not the same.
That matters not.

Each has traveled a journey
of thousands of miles.

And each viewed not
according to their journey,
yet viewed with eyes
that flow from the heart.

A heart that knows the two
are connected,
viewed with eyes flowing
from the heart that only
knows unconditional love.

Eyes wide open to
the Truth of each one's journey.

The Truth that judgment of another is
simply a reflection of judgment
held within one towards oneself.

There is a space within,
a space that was once filled with
the darkness of judgment.

A space that is now
free for compassion
and love for one's self and others.

Space to breathe easier
Space to live easier
Space to live peacefully
Space to allow all to BE
and travel the paths chosen.

There's a space within.
A Beautiful Space.

May we all release
and expose this space within
for the Beauty it reveals.

March 2018

This poem flowed forth from the below words I had written at a different time regarding judgments and compassion. For some reason I saved them. After the above poem flowed through me, I knew why.

"……. The space within me that held the weight of so many judgments …

Judgments against people who thought, felt, and looked differently, judgments against single moms, judgments against parents whose kids act out and the kids too.

Every single time one of those judgments was released, a cushion of compassion took its place. There are still some wee judgments hiding in there.

Some that stay hidden and some that peek out to see if it's safe. Within me is not a safe zone for judgments. You are released and a warm, soft, loving cushion of compassion takes your place."

Listen, Trust, Jump

And she listened,
And listened,
And listened.

And she heard,
Write.
Write.
Write.

And she knew,
The time was
Approaching
For her to jump.

The time was
Nearing for her
To leap into
Her soul's purpose.

And so she
Remained still.

And she listened,
And listened,
And listened.

Nearly time.
Dear One,
BE ready.

February 2018

Unfolding of Time

Can I?

The changes.
Create fear,
they do.

We're all getting older,
life is not as it was.

What is this strange
thing happening?

It is true things change,
nothing stays the same.

What is happening?

Can I handle the changes?

It's all changing
I'm changing
they are changing
nothing is as it was.

There's no stopping
the changes.

It's the one thing
we can be sure will
arrive – changes.

Why do the changes
create such suffering?
Why do the changes
have to be experienced
in isolation ... loneliness?

Why does one allow
the mind to create such
suffering with the changes?

Why can one not
be in the midst
of the changes
and simply shift
one's perspective?

That's not how
it is anymore.
Got it.
Let's move forward.

Why can this not be
done with releasing
that which was and is
no longer?

Why does the change
seem to have suffering
as its sidekick?

Can I handle the changes
happening in my life?

Why does one crave
Sameness?

Why does one want
the comfort of
knowing how it
is to be?

Why does one
want to experience
change with
another by their side?

Can I handle the changes
of my life?

What other path
is there?

Embrace the change
Shift one's perspective
Go with the flow
And know one is truly not alone.

Or

Resist the change,
want what is no longer,
and create suffering
for oneself and those
the one loves.

I know what this
heart chooses
And will never forget
what the heart will
always choose.

Every morning meditation
and in every moment
this is the place
I will attempt to Be.

Give up, I will not …..

Embrace
Shift
Go with the flow
And know.

Come my child
Let it Go.

This is the Way
of non-suffering.

December 2017

Vastness

One breath at a time, dear one

You find yourself in a vast ocean of your own creation.
An ocean full of the humanness of life.
Joy, love, peace,
laughter, happiness, abundance,
beauty, compassion, kindness.
Fear, sadness, greed,
competition, judgments, shame,
guilt, jealousy, loneliness.

At times you feel as if you
are on the verge of drowning.

One's arms and legs have become
heavy with the struggle of this
ocean swirling with humanness.

What is one to do?
There is no place to return.

You jumped in knowing
there was only One Way to survive
in this vast ocean of humanness.
One breath at a time.

For as you breathe each breath
it is another opportunity
to feel the humanness of life.

Feel all of it,
the comforting and
the unlovely,
and then release it into
the vast ocean to be
cleansed by Mother Earth.

For one day you will feel
the heavy burden begin to
lift from your arms and legs.

You will know only the
unconditional love of this
ocean of humanness.

All the rest is still there.
Yes, it is.
Still swim in it, you do.

Yet, it just brushes by you
as you are drenched in the
unconditional love of all that is.

Rather than struggle
You move in harmony
with the humanness.

One breath at a time,
See, there it is ...
You just took another breath and another
and another ...

Keep breathing, Keep swimming
in this vast ocean and know
you are not alone.

You are surrounded and uplifted
by the One Love and breathe
it in with each breath.

You cannot escape the One Love.
It is always with you.

One breath at a time.

December 2017

Shining Star Bag

You can take
All the hearts
Nature puts forth

And put them
All in a bag
Made of stars
Wrapped in a
Bow of beautiful
Green grass.

But there'll be
Days when no
Matter the beauty
No matter the love
No matter the
Depth of knowing
How the Light
Shines within.

There'll be days
When a heaviness
Envelops and that
Shining star bag
Full of love means.

Absolutely nothing.

There'll be days
When the sweetness
And beauty of
Every breath
Is not felt nor seen.

Yet, these days
Shall pass.
These days
Shall pass.

Pass, they shall.
And waiting will
Be that shining star
Bag of hearts
And love.

For Nature is
Patient.
Nature is ever there
With love and light.

Love,
The Seed Pod

December 2017

Whisperings of the Heart

The heart whispers secrets
Try not to hear it you do.

Continuing to be in the game of life
Following the rules, filling out the papers,
conforming to the this-is-the-way-it's-done norms.
Too busy for interruption
to hear the gentle whisperings of the heart.

Yet, the whisperings never fully quiet.
They are there.
The whisperings are ever delivered
with love and gentleness.

The whisperings of the heart judge not.
The whisperings of the heart
are patient and steady.

Ever so gently the whisperings continue
to impart the truth of one's soul.

At times the whisperings grow louder
At times they are heard with deeper clarity.

In youth the whisperings were strong
and vibrant with a deep knowing.

As the years passed the whisperings
were quieted by the outside world.

As the seconds pass
as the minutes pass
as the hours pass
as the days pass
as the months pass
as the years pass
as the decades pass

Ever faithful and resilient
the whisperings settle into the
unconditional love of one's heart.

Awaiting the precious time
to once again whisper the
knowings of one's soul.

That time does indeed arrive.
Uninvited, invited,
unexpected, expected.
With struggle, with joy
With peace, with pain.
Yet, it does arrive.

The veil of illusion
begins to lift.
The whisperings of the heart
awaken to the light allowed
to penetrate.

Begin to listen, one does.
Listen with clarity.
Listen with knowing.

Listen with deep understanding.
Begin to take action, one does.

Yet, many times still ignoring
the whisperings of the heart.
The pull of the way life is
supposed to BE lived is strong.

It arrives.
It brings enlightenment.
The day of realizing the
whisperings of the heart
bear the key
to one's freedom to live
and serve as one has always known
one was meant to BE.

Free to sing the song
of one's soul.
Free to step out of the
board game of conformity
Free to shine the Pure Light
the whisperings of the heart
have always shone from within.

Free to share Divine
Unconditional love
to all beings.
Free to listen and live
the whisperings of the heart.

November 2017

Memory Lane

Why did the beautiful and fun
memories hurt so badly
Why did her chest feel
heavy and her stomach in knots

The place where she and
her children had spent
seven years of their lives.

The place where her son
spent his young life
from one year old
through eight years old.

Driving past the many sidewalks
and the trail where she had taken
walks alone, walks with
just her son, and walks
together as a family.

Driving past the home
her parents had lived,
the home she and her kids had lived,
the second home her parents had lived.

Remembering neighbors she had
chatted with. Remembering
the spread of holiday cheer.

Oh, the pain, the pain.

Why do such wonderful
memories hurt her heart.

Why does she feel
a sense of loss
no longer living
in this neighborhood.
No longer having
her parents living
in the same neighborhood.

Why does she feel
like nothing turned
out as she had wanted.

Why does she feel
like she has failed
her children in
not providing them
with the same kind
of home that they
loved so much
in their early childhood?

Why does she feel
like she has given up?
Why do the tears flow
in mourning something
that never really was?

She keeps reminding
herself that nothing
is permanent. The
only thing that's
permanent is change
Itself.

She reminds herself
that home is truly
where the heart is.
Yet, what if the
heart is closed and
doesn't want to hear
these things.

What if she reminds
herself that none of
it seems to have gone as
she wanted it to go,
the way she dreamed
it would.

Seems as if she
has been but
a piece of sand
in a vast ocean
of life tossing
her here and there
into this experience
and that experience.

She thinks she should
not return to this
place if it is so
painful …

but then she knows
she must keep returning
until she has felt
all the pain there
is to feel, for in
feeling the pain and
being with the pain
loving the pain
embracing the pain
is she assured
of the joy and beauty
that awaits her
on the other side
of the pain.

She may not have
fully let herself
feel the pain at the time
she and her children
had to leave their
home and neighborhood.

Brushed it under
the heart she did.
Believing she did not have to feel the pain.
She knows she let herself feel

some of the pain.
Yet, there is more there.

She makes a new
commitment to continue
to visit this neighborhood
until she has let herself
feel every single bit
of grief, guilt, and sadness
there is to feel.

She will feel it, feel the
aches in her chest, feel
the knots in her stomach
feel and taste the salty tears as
they stream down her face.

She reflects back on
these times as some of
the happiest of her
and her children's lives.

So carefree and joyful.
Doing many things together
as a family, many adventures,
every trip in the car an adventure.

It seems those times are no longer.
Where have they gone? The kids are
no longer kids. One a teenager and
one a preteen. Change.

Change is the nature
of life. This season of autumn
reminds us always that this
is how it flows. Change.

Why did she grip so tightly
to that time in her life,
in her kids' lives?

Why does she not want to
let it go? Why does she
remember it with longing?

Why does she feel lost
in shifting to this
new normal for her
and her kids?

Interests have shifted.
What was fun and exciting
is no longer.

How does she go with the
flow, with the change,
without clinging to the
Past?

She does it one breath
at a time. One blink at
at time. One step at a
time. One gratitude
thought at a time.

One act of kindness
at a time. One smile
at a time.

With kindness and
love directed to herself
and her heart.

She does it by observing
and not letting herself
get caught in the spiral
of emotions. Be with them,
feel them, and let them
release to reveal the new
normal. As it will only
be the new normal for a short
time. That is the nature
of life.

For life will support
in whatever stage of
life one finds one's self.

Nature is the Divine's
Gift to allow one to
experience change and
the cyclical nature
of life outside of
One's self, yet still,
it is within as we are
one with nature.

Be still. Feel the emotions.
Let them pass through
like the wind passes
through the autumn leaves.
And know.
This is life.
And we are always
supported and loved.

November 2017

Lead the Way

I know not what I am doing.

This requires more than
self-confidence could ever provide.

This beckons a confidence not of my self.

A confidence ruled by the force
that causes the musk thistle to do what it does.
Sprout, grow, bloom, wither, blow
with the wind, and reseed.

The force that holds the stars
in the sky and the same force
that grew two beings in my womb.

This beckons a confidence not of my self.

A confidence that compels one
to put aside one's personal preferences
and what one thinks one wants.

A strong force, it is.

Nature shows us how.

Be still.
Let go.
Surrender to not knowing.

And let the One confidence lead the Way.

November 2017

Continue

Create what is in your heart.
Share it with others.
You are coming home.
Yes, you are.
You may take detours,
Yet, you are on your way.
Listen to the voice of nature,
the voice of the divine.
I will not lead you astray.

You successfully live
as a human on this beautiful
Mother Earth when you
share and create from the heart.
That is love. It is good.
My voice arises
from the heart.
All that I am is Good.
All that I am is Love.
You are Good.
You are Love.
You are. I am.

Embrace with love the
voice of the inner critic.
The more you practice
the easier it will become.

The magical day will dawn
when the inner critic
melts into and blossoms
to the Divine love
which is you.

Place focus in the heart.
Go forth from this divine space.
Love the voice of the inner critic.
Continue dear one.
Continue,
And know that
You are never judged
And always loved.
I love you.

August 2017

Walk With Me

Come,
Walk with me.

Do you not see,
that you have
tethered yourself
to illusions.
That create the
suffering you experience.

The illusion that you
are small,
that you must
compete and attack
to survive.

An illusion that comes
not from your soul.
Your soul knows the truth.

When you feel bliss,
when you feel time
stand still,
When you are truly joyful,
When you know that all is well,
When you look into
the eyes of another
and see the universe.
When you give and receive
love to yourself,

your brothers and sisters,
animals and Mother Earth.

These are when you have
let illusions fall away
and experience the
Truth of Grandeur.

Practice, you must,
at walking into the
confusion, overwhelm,
and fear for these are
not of the Truth.

For only when you
release the tethered
cord of illusion
will you be set free.

Come,
Walk with Me
And come home
to the Truth.

July 2017

Path of the Heart

Allowing oneself
to be pulled in
many directions, you are.

From task to task you move,
As confusion, anxiety,
and worry enter the thoughts.

Let go, you must.
Be aware.
Listen to the
heart message.

Know this.
When riddled with questions,
plagued by confusion,
and held hostage by anxiety,
This is not of the heart.

Distractions, these are,
to cover the message
of the heart,
to prevent one
Following the
Path of the heart.

As distractions enter
Consciousness,
Always come back
to the knowing

of this message.

Let go, you must.
Listen to the now,
Listen not to the past.

The path of
the heart will emerge.
While distractions
to Mother Earth purge.

July 2017

Shadows

Do you see?

Slipped into the shadows
of your being, you have.
When sadness and lack
have settled within.
When comparison of
oneself with others
is the theme
of the day.

When appreciation
has faded and the
heart tightly closed,
you can be sure
the shadows have appeared.

When the light has
dimmed and you feel
smothered by the shadows.
Welcome the light back,
you can.

Remember all the times
Of living in the light
All the times of
joy and freedom.
All the times of
abundance and peace.
They are there too.

Do not forget them.

Remember those times
not with longing,
for this causes the
distance greater.
Remember those times
knowing they are
still there
simply awaiting
your return.

These thoughts are
the bridge that
connect the light
and darkness.
Comfortable you
are in the suffering
of the darkness.

The first
step onto the bridge
out of darkness
is the most
difficult step.

My gift to you
if you choose to see …

Life is a dance
with the light
and the shadows.

The dance of shadows cannot
be a dance sat out
if true freedom and peace
is the destination you seek.

For when you take the time
to dance with the shadows
with curiosity and patience
You will see that all of
life is a dance of contrast.

Have patience when
dancing with the shadows
of your being.

Love both the light and shadows
for one cannot
exist without the other.

Allow yourself to be free
and dance with me.

June 2017

Heart Song

Sweet one,
Be with me
For a moment.

I ask of you
Out of your mind
To venture.

Come forth
Into your heart.
Listen to the song
Of the heart.
For she sings
A love song
Sweet and beautiful.

A song designed
Specifically for you.
Hear you will not,
If you choose
To live life
Only in the realm of the mind.

The mind is a tool
To be used in
Unison with the
The song of the heart.

Come forth into
Your heart.
Listen to the song
Of the heart.
Live life from
The music of the heart

And set yourself free.

Love,
The Flowering Bush

December 2016

The Place

Come, Be with me.

You are drawn
to me for a reason.

There is a time
and a season
for all that you
will remember.

You will experience
a pivotal life shift,
That opens the portal
to divine knowing.

The place you
finally allow
yourself to rest.

To prepare for
the sharing of
divine love
in a way
only you can share.

The mind is quieted,
Let what must fall away.
Removing yourself
from the many
directions you

have strayed.

All to come forth
as you came here
to come forth,
Sharing divine love.

Come. Be with me.

Love,
The Grain of Sand

June 2017

Dear Tree,

At times when I look at you,
I'm instantly taken to the
Heart of knowing
That we are friends.
You and I, oh yes,
Friends for an eternity.
Friends, lovers, siblings,
Parents, cousins, and
Everything in between.
We are all of these
And stardust and
Moonbeams too. Oh yes.
An eternity, oh yes.

Fall 2016

Grow With Me

Go, Hurry, Hurry
Go, Hurry, Hurry
This is the mantra
You help me to release.

Stop, Slow, Slow
Stop, Slow, Slow
This is the mantra
You share with me.

Be quiet. Be still.
Listen. Be in silence.
Communicate without words.
Communicate from the divine heart.

Watch me. Learn with me.
Lean on me.
Ask of me assistance.
Grow with me.
We have much to learn
from one another.

Let us be the
Connected ones
We came here to BE.
Let us share divine love
In our own unique ways.

Fall 2016

Walking

Walking is spiritual.
Walking is magical.
Walking is miraculous.
Walking is praying.
Walking is meditation.
Walking awakens one from the deep sleep of separation.
Walking is dancing with the oneness of all that is.

Fall 2016

Sunbeams

With you by my side,
I am grace.

With you by my side,
I am grateful.

With you by my side,
I am never alone.

With you by my side,
I am free to be me.

May 2017

Eye to Eye with the Tree

Your limbs higher than
can be conceived.
Evokes within,
a primal urge
to lift my limbs
as yours,
while feelings of knowing
brew and bubble deep
within the very depths of my soul.

With limbs lifted,
Eyes gently closed,
The lips are parted
and out flows the breath
and feeling of the all knowing,
all one, divine love.

Standing next to you,
Eye to eye,
Standing next to you,
We feel our oneness.

April 2017

Mountain Trail

You know me so well,
Mirroring life as it is lived.

Sometimes up,
Sometimes down.

And sometimes the journey
is smooth and level.

Oh, beautiful Mother Earth
We make a great team.

Mirroring for one another
Verily, verily, we make a great ONE.

Fall 2016

Life of the Tree

Like a gentle breeze
Moves through you,
You move through
The clouds of my soul,
Revealing the truth
Obscured by living
A life of illusion.
By the grace of You
I can see clearly now.

Fall 2016

Learning

Walks of clarity
Walks of peace
Walking for no reason
Walking to get nowhere
This is the walking
Of which I speak and write.
These are the walks
That become what
One most needs
In the moment.
The walking becomes
The teacher and
Nature the classroom.

Fall 2016

Wanderer

A wandering I shall go
Your beauty entices me
Deeper and deeper
I must go.
For time spent
with you is cleansing.
As water rinses the dirt
from this body, so
You rinse the
mind and body
of illusions
Step after step
your beauty mixes love with the intellect
For what is the intellect alone
if not first passed
through the heart of divine love.

Fall 2016

The Heart Knows

The eye cannot
Conceive the miracle
It beholds.
The beauty surpasses
The knowing of
The senses.
The heart knows.
Hallelujah!
The heart knows.
The heart remembers
How to fly
Into the mystic.
Delivering remembrance
To every cell
Returning us to
and revealing the oneness
Of all.

Fall 2016

Harmony of the Wild Flowers

The world slows
Time nearly stops
And I see.
I see your differences
I see the contrast.
I see what you impart.
You shine light
Upon the harmony of nature
So that I may see the
Oneness of nature and
The oneness of humanity
I am held in your loving
Embrace to have the all of all
Poured into my open heart.
And I say, yes, I see, and
I will share and shine the light.

Fall 2016

All of Life

One with sun,
One with moon,
One with water,
One with trees,
One with soil,
One with wind,
One with birds and bees,
One with rain,
One with fire,
One with me,
One with all of life,
One with love.

Fall 2016

Show Me

Great Spirit,

With Your
Grace and guidance
Show me with pure eyes
Let me hear with clarity.

Guide me in the knowing
Of the Way I am
To share Divine Love.

Gently open my heart
To reveal the fire of
Passion that burns within.

For every day is a chance
To begin again,
A chance to live and love.

Winter 2016

Vibrant

Living life with wild abandon
Bursting with vibrancy
In every direction
Being joyful to be you.
Oh tree! You inspire me.
To live life in this way,
Is to live free.

December 2016

Grow

Grow where you are,
Lest you spend precious time
Waiting to grow
Until you arrive someplace else.
For when one reaches the
Someplace else, there will
Always be the next someplace else.
Grow as your heart desires
from within,
To allow without to miraculously
Support one's growth.

Love,
The Tree Roots

December 2016

Without

The delicate balance
Of life and death.
Without life
There is no death
Without death
There is no life
Death is life and
Life is death.

Love,
The Dying Flower

December 2016

We

To go with the flow,
To be at ease,
To live in harmony,
This is you
And this is me.

Love,
The San Antonio River

December 2016

Inspired Peace

Trunks and branches growing in opposite directions,
all with different views. Yet, you are eternally at peace.
Oh tree. You inspire me.

November 2016

Beauty of the Tree

You are perfect.
Every shadow.
Every line.
Every bump.
Every curve.
You are perfectly divine.
My eyes could study you for an eternity
and still not grasp the depths of your beauty.
My heart need not study you at all.
For the heart knows the depths of your beauty.
Our beauty is one and the same.
We are perfect.

November 2016

Nature's Freedom

The depth of your beauty,
It pours into the bowels of the soul.
Cleansing the soul of clouds
that shadow the knowing.
To be free, to love, to know.

August 2016

Nature's Classroom

The one supporting the many,
The many supporting the one,
This interdependent relationship you share
A lost art to we.

It's clear to see,
The disconnect coming forth,
When the wild is taken from you,
Mirrored in the forests
Of the society of we.

Oh Mother, what a sweet
And beautiful teacher you Be.

Fall 2016

Reflection

Just as my internal world seems a marsh of confusion and brokenness at times,
I see clearly you experience and mirror the same.
Let's be still in togetherness as the marsh clears and rejoice in the tenderness of life.

September 2016

Weeds

To bend and bow,
to be flexible,
to be strong
to be resilient,
This is me,
and this is you.

September 2016

Musk Thistle

When I truly see you,
I see me,
I see love,
I see the pulsing wheel of life
that connects us all.

October 2016

Blooming Rose

When I'm tired, you lift me.
When my thoughts have settled on sadness,
you hold a gentle space for me.
You remind me to unfold with life
and help me remember to simply be.

October 2016

Stillness

With each breath I take,
With each step I take,
Your stillness greets me.
A stillness that whispers
the language of oneness and peace.

October 2016

Secrets of Nature

Deeper and deeper I must go,
your secrets I must know.
Your presence delivers unbounded clarity.
Your embrace awakens the ability
to listen with an open heart,
to hear the secrets you share.

September 2016

Nature's Peace

The moment I enter your embrace,
my shoulders relax,
my neck softens,
I breathe deeply,
and I know I'm home.

August 2016

Tree Power

All that you witness I may never know.
Your strength is my strength.
Your patience reminds.
Your flexibility inspires.
As we dance this life together I reveal your beauty to you,
and you reveal my beauty to me.
Shall we dance?

August 2016

The Alchemy of Gratitude

A Walk in February

Graceful trees
Bright blue sky
Soft fluffy snow
Gratitude blossoms

February 2019

Glorious Water

Water, glorious water.

Oh, how I am grateful.

Grateful,
for you are life,
You help to create life,
You sustain life,
YOU are everything to life.

I bless you and am
eternally grateful
for the blessings
you bestow.

You uplift,
You inspire,
You clean,
You refresh,
You quench,
You sustain,
YOU are simply amazing.

Water, dear water
I vow to be ever
more mindful of
your presence,
ever more mindful
to bless you,
ever more mindful

of being grateful
that you BE.

I Am grateful for water.
Bless you Water.
I Am.

March 2018

Honoring Water on World Water Day

Nature's Abundance

I feel the frosty cold
embrace as You brush
across this body.
I feel and Know
your Abundance.

I touch and hug
the beautiful,
scarred and knotted
trees that sprout
and grow from Your soil.
I feel and Know
your Abundance.

I delight in the sparkling
and unique snowflakes
as they drift from
the brooding clouds
above and lightly fall
upon this body.
I feel and Know
your Abundance.

Lo, even as I dodge
and walk through
the nuggets of
geese waste left
behind by these
majestic and
interesting creatures,

I feel and Know
your Abundance.

Yes, I feel Your abundance
I Know it now.

It's been a long road
getting to this
glorious and bountiful place.
Yet, I have arrived.

I have arrived
to the freedom
of Knowing this …

I am made of bits
and pieces of You.
You are made of
bits and pieces of me.
This body and soul
mix with Your essence
as we collide.

I see it now.
All that is made
of You is Good.
ALL, I say, ALL!

Even as your form is
changed and no longer
resembles Your essence.
It is of You.

And, it is Good.

Humans take and borrow
from you to create,
grow, and make
the things we must
have to survive,
yet, also the things
we think we need,
and the things we
simply want so
as to fill a void.
Grateful for your
abundance and gifts
I am.

We take your trees
and metals and we
make this mysterious
and sometimes elusive
thing called money.

We make it into
something it is not.
It is only of
You and we use it
for good, for bad,
for our benefit,
and for the benefit
of others.

One slight shift

in awareness of
what money truly is ..

That is True Freedom.
Freedom to respect
and love that money
stuff of which
contains Your essence.

Knowing, absorbing
and feeling
Your abundance
has brought on
this shift from
lack to abundance.

Thank You
Mother Earth.
Thank You
Nature.

I feel and Know
your Abundance.
You are Abundance.
I Am Abundance.
And so it is.
I Am.

March 2018

Appreciation

Notice nature.
Feel and smell the air.
Study the clouds and the trees.
Listen to the birds.
How many different kinds of songs can you hear?
What kinds of birds are they?
Enjoy a sunset.
Notice and smell freshly bloomed flowers.
Notice and study new buds on a tree.
Notice the smell of newly fallen leaves.
Study the moon, stars, and clouds.
Walk barefoot in the grass, dirt, or sand.
Watch the waves in the ocean,
Or the ripple in a lake,
Or the rushing water of a river.
Notice the glimmer of freshly fallen snow.
Watch the sunlight dance and sparkle on the water.
Study the trees.
Get up close. Touch them.
Go for a walk for no reason other than to commune with nature.

Fall 2016

Beauty

A sense of wonder
Within is awakened
As I admire your beauty.

Imparting your beauty
To you, and mine to me.

To live with wonder
To live with beauty
To live with knowing

This is our divine gift
To one another.

December 2016

Open the Heart

Nature knows not
Her beauty without us.
We know not
Our beauty, compassion,
And peace without her.
Oh beautiful tree
The lessons thou impart to me
Open the heart to be free
Grateful to you
I will forever be.

Fall 2016

The Alchemy of Fun

The Italian Named Frank

Always ready
To celebrate
And to do it
With flair!

Good food and drink
He's ever happy
To serve it up.

Willing to help,
Ready to give hugs,
With much love.

One who can
Be counted on
To bring along
The silly side
Of any holiday!

With Christmas classics,
Moose mugs and
Leg lamps,
Sealed with a kiss
Underneath the mistletoe.

Love,
Camilla
xoxo

December 2018

Dedicated to my step-father, Frank Romano.

Ode to Patty

Always there,
Always with
Love to share.

Always with a
Comfy and cozy
House to share.

She makes
Us giggle
She makes
Us wiggle ...

She makes us wiggle?
Well, not really, yet
That's the word
That shot forth!

Deeply for her
Family she
Does care.

Always there,
Always with
Love to share.

Love,
Camilla
xoxo

December 2018

Dedicated to my mom, Patty Romano.

Ode to the Sock

Sock, Oh Sock!
What a strange
creature you are!

Your creation was
meant for good
I can see that.

Yet, most times you come
equipped with a built-in
irritator to rub
these precious feet.

Rub, rub, rub in a way
that the mind latches onto.
Latches onto and will not
let go until we remove
the offending creature
from our feet.

That seam!
That seam
makes us want
to scream!

Sock, Oh Sock!

We simply want our toes
and feet to be free.
Free from the

confines of your
Scratchy
Stringy
Strangling
Materials.

We do enjoy the softness
and warmth you provide
when needed.

Yet, most times
we would rather
you Be anywhere else
but confining our feet.

Sock, Oh Sock!

We send you love.
Yet, send you on your way.

Here's to Toe and Foot Freedom …

September 2018

Dedicated to my youngest child, Thomas, as one who asks, "Am I the only one that wears socks inside out?" And, one who has also commented, "The people who make socks, make them wrong."

The Circle of Life

On a bed of lentils,
surrounded by yellow flowers,
in cycles of three
she rotated through life.

What has she done wrong,
What did she do for all
the right reasons?
Haunted her it has,
ever since.

Hold the faith in I AM,
she will.
Knowing her inner beauty,
using the dark spaces to grow.

Pulling old roots,
Planting new roots.
Never forgetting how
lovely she is.
Don't forget the tomatoes!

She lost her voice,
building a shield
to protect herself.

The time is now to
gently lower the shield.
To release her Voice.
Knowing her self-worth,

Knowing her value,
Loving herself.

Lord Ganesha and Goddess Kali,
Are you here yet?

Here comes the Gust
of Cheer!
How's the lipstick?
You Ain't Seen Nothing Yet!

August 2018

Inspired by a conversation with my dear friend Lalita Simon.
This is a poetry soup of our conversation.

Dance

Beautiful blossoms
for a beautiful tree
As we reflect our beauty
upon one another
You make me feel like dancing.

October 2016

Love is Magical

Cows are loud and can moo
sometimes they say,
I love you!

Cows have milk,
and cows eat grass.

You are surrounded by love
every breath you take is love
You are love

Guinea pigs wheek and guinea pigs meek,
lovey dovey guinea piggy moo!

Love is the butterfly
gracefully it flies
magical is its color

Love is magical
the alchemy of peace.

Airplanes flying
through the air
fun galore!

How beautiful the bird flies,
as the wind.

Love is the tree
Love is the flower
Love is the silence.

Flowers blossom
pollen falls.

Rainbow is the sky
Rainbow is the water
Rainbow is the colors of the earth.

Nature is love
Nature knows how to be.

Team TLC
always kind
always thinking.

Kindness is always there
Kindness is like friendship

A wise man
is kind to the kind
and kind to the unkind

A wise man
under a tree

Blue bird flies to Alaska
Red bird flies to Hawaii
White bird flies to Australia

The magical hummingbird
arrives on a warm summer day

Sushi
best food ever
try some

Pineapple
Most delicious food ever

Mindful eating
Mindful living
The way of peace and happiness

Eating is fun
and yummy

Apple trees grow with sunshine
Butterflies grow with food
Cake gets eaten fast or slow.

Beings, trees, and insects
We are all one love.

July 2015

A Renga poem written by Team TLC ... Thomas Darnell, Lillian Darnell, and Camilla Downs. Thomas wrote the first stanza, Lillian the second, and Camilla the third. We rotated in that order until the completion of the poem.

Closing

Thank you for spending your precious time on the pages of this book. It is my deepest wish, having spent time together through these writings, that you feel a sense of camaraderie and knowing that you are not alone.

It is also my deepest wish that you have a go at writing. If you aren't accustomed to writing, it may take time to grease the writing wheels. Don't give up. Try it for at least a month. No one has to see what you write. Delete it, tear it up, shred it, crumple and stomp on it, burn it, eat it, whatever.

Write. Write and watch the transformation of becoming a more connected and focused human. Not only that. Write and watch the transformation as you begin to trust yourself and become more at peace with life.

With all my love,

Camilla

About the Author

Camilla Downs is a bestselling author, indie publisher, mentor, and mom. Nature and life experiences are a constant source of inspiration for her writing. She enjoys living a minimalist lifestyle, practicing meditation and mindfulness, reading, going for walks, and capturing nature's essence with photographs. Camilla is the founder of MeetingtheAuthors.com and lives in Northern Nevada with her two kids and their pet guinea pig.

Her first book, *D iz for Different - One Woman's Journey to Acceptance*, published in 2012 reached #1 in Special Needs Parenting and #2 in Self-Help on Amazon.

She and her two kids call themselves Team TLC; "T" for Thomas, "L" for Lillian, "C" for Camilla. This began in the year 2009 as Camilla sensed her family needed something to bring them together. Team TLC worked perfectly as they all embraced it, referring to themselves using Team TLC, and even receiving mail addressed to Team TLC.

Lillian Darnell just celebrated her 18th birthday and has a condition known as 18p-. This means she is missing the short arm of chromosome number 18; which happened spontaneously in utero. 18p- manifests for her with speech difficulties in articulating letters and words, balance and depth perception issues, chronic pain, extreme fears, inability to make decisions, and struggles with processing difficult emotions. Lillian was unschooled (similar to homeschooling) and graduated on June 1, 2019. She is an artist and writer, with her debut book, *Where Would You Fly and Other Magical Stories*, published in 2018.

Thomas Darnell recently celebrated his 14th birthday. He is unschooled and has about four more years of schooling before he graduates. Thomas enjoys having philosophical and political discussions and is a fan of the Star Wars and Marvel movies. His favorite composer is John Williams. Thomas is also an avid computer gamer. His first book, *Biggest Little Photographer*, was published in 2016.

Connect with Camilla:

CamillaDowns.com
MeetingtheAuthors.com
TheTeamTLC.com
facebook.com/CamillaDownsAuthor
instagram.com/CamillaDowns
twitter.com/CamillaDowns

The Chromosome 18 Registry & Research Society is an advocacy organization composed primarily of the parents of individuals with a chromosome 18 abnormality. We consist of three separate organizations located in the United States, Australia, and Europe, all with a common mission: To help people with chromosome 18 abnormalities overcome the obstacles they face so they may lead healthy and productive lives. We are proud to count among our members those who are affected by chromosome 18 abnormalities, extended family members, and medical professionals. Membership is open to any interested person. We are a 501(c)(3) non-profit, tax-exempt public charity.

Our work is supported by individual donations and charitable foundations. We have met the strict criteria for fiscal responsibility set by the Combined Federal Campaign.

Identifying Treatments for Chromosome 18 Conditions

The Chromosome 18 Clinical Research Center is dedicated to understanding and developing treatments for chromosome 18 conditions. To accomplish these goals, Chromosome 18 Registry & Research Society collects data on the natural progression of the chromosome 18 conditions, studies the key genes responsible for those features, and identifies drugs that can regulate those genes. With the help of our over 4000 members, The Chromosome 18 Research Center will continue progressing towards our goals.

Information courtesy of The Chromosome 18 Registry and Research Society. To learn more visit Chromosome18.org.

Nature is magical
Nature is raw beauty
Nature is pure therapy

Camilla Downs

www.ingramcontent.com/pod-product-compliance
Lightning Source LLC
Chambersburg PA
CBHW050631300426
44112CB00012B/1753